FROM BASTARD
TO BELOVED

HEALING THE VOID OF THE FATHERLESS

Shaunta Jones

Copyright © December 2024 Shaunta Jones

All rights reserved. This document is geared towards providing exact and reliable information about the topic and issue covered. The publication is sold because the publisher is not required to render accounting, officially permitted, or qualified services. If advice is necessary, legal or professional, a practiced individual in the profession should be ordered.

No part of this publication may be reproduced, duplicated, distributed, or transmitted in any form or by any means, including photocopying, recording, or other electronic or mechanical methods, without the prior written permission of the publisher, except in the case of brief quotations embodied in critical reviews and certain other noncommercial uses permitted by copyright law. Recording this publication is strictly prohibited and any storage of this document is not allowed unless with written permission from the publisher. All rights reserved.

The information provided herein is stated to be truthful and consistent, in that any liability, in terms of inattention or otherwise, by any usage or abuse of any policies, processes, or directions contained within is the solitary and utter responsibility of the recipient reader. Under no circumstances will any legal responsibility or blame be held against the publisher for any reparation, damages, or monetary loss due to the information herein, either directly or indirectly.

Respective authors own all copyrights not held by the publisher.

Printed by Kiyanni B., Write It Out Publishing, LLC. in the United States of America.

Write It Out Publishing LLC
Virginia Beach, Virginia
Writeitoutpublishing.com

ISBN: 979-8-9919982-6-0

Book Cover Illustrator: By Author
Editor: Tamira Butler-Likely

First printing, (e-book or paperback) December 2024
Author Shaunta Jones
Charlotte, NC
info@shauntaspeaks.com
shauntaspeaks.com

TABLE OF CONTENTS

Foreword	vii
A Loving Note from Your Heavenly Father	ix
Introduction	xi
Chapter I: Plague of Unforgiveness	1
Chapter II: Love	7
Chapter III: Forgive	17
Chapter IV: Release	25
Chapter V: Good Grief	39
Chapter VI: Driving Force	47
Chapter VII: Lost Childhood	55
Chapter VIII: No More	59
Chapter IX: Healed to Heal	65
Chapter X: Child of God	71
Conclusion	79
About the Author	81
A Prayer for You: (Say Aloud)	82
Prayer Points and Prophetic Decrees	83

Dedication

To my beloved mother, Rev. Azaline H. Simmons, although I miss your physical presence, I'm grateful you gave me your blessing on writing this book prior to your heavenly promotion. I hope I'm still making you proud as I strive to adhere to your number one life lesson: knowing who I am and whose I am. Thank you for portraying what a life as a child of God looks like.

To my amazing husband, Z. Antoine, your love has both grounded and elevated me. Watching you with our children has been the cathartic catalyst that has administered a healing balm to my deepest wounds. Thank you for being my launching pad and safe place to land. You and the kids are God's greatest blessings to me.

And to my children, Micaylah, Azaliah Grace, Zachary Jr., Immanuel Anthony, and Zoe Victoria, may you always know that you are the driving force behind all I do. It's an honor to be your mom.

Foreword

My whole life has been dedicated to helping others overcome the challenges of being fatherless. When I was given this opportunity to write this foreword, I was honored by the author to read this amazing work that really hits close to home. *From Bastard to Beloved: "Healing the Void of the Fatherless"* has different challenges that many are facing currently in life without having the answers to overcome the void of not being accepted and feeling alone without having the love of your father to support you.

This book will address rejection of a father, dealing with the spirit of abandonment, and overcoming low self-esteem issues that were caused by a failed relationship with your father. The author, Shaunta Jones, will take you step-by-step to cover many of her own challenges and how she overcame the pain of rejection.

In this book, it shows you the polarity of pain to healing. As a Senior Pastor, I had many parishioners who dealt with the rejection of their father, and this abandonment is a serious void that can cause an onset of other difficulties in loving yourself as well as looking for others to love you like you've imagined your father should have.

As you read this amazing book, I highly recommend taking time to meditate on each chapter which gives you biblical insight on how to overcome this void, and it will help you to receive healing to be whole in God's word to move forward in living your life without pain and enjoy the plans God has for you.

It was hard for me to put this book down when I started reading it, and in my time of reflection it brought back some of my own personal memories that I have overcome through forgiveness. Remember to apply each chapter's recommendations to your life from the Word of God to get the wisdom that is needed to help you to be an overcomer too.

Sammie Lee Wagner Jr., Senior Pastor New Foundation Church International Charlotte, NC

A Loving Note from Your Heavenly Father

My Dear Child,

I know your journey through this world may not be what you would call ideal. I know you have questions and hurts that run deep.

I am here for you. You can come to me with your angry inquisitions and most dreadful misconceptions. Nothing is hidden from me, so there's no need to try to fix yourself up before inviting me in.

In me is the joy you so desperately need and uncontainable rapids of peace that will overtake you and bring you to your knees, redefining, replenishing, reviving you in every way.

There is nothing that can be done about the past but for you to choose to see it from my point of view. You've analyzed it from your perspective long enough; now it's time to take my hand and allow me to reveal to you the truth.

Your birth was My will, but your rebirth has to be your choice. To be born again doesn't mean you'll get to erase all the harmful things that have happened, but it does mean those things will no longer have a hold on you.

There's nothing more that I want for you than to be free.

The days ahead may be filled with challenges, but as a child of mine, I'll equip you with the tools you need to overcome anything that comes your way. Let's exchange what was for the beauty of what could be. They're not really insurmountable challenges, actually. Instead, look at them as circumstances orchestrated for you to seek, trust, and know me.

I long for a relationship with you. I yearn to be your guiding light. I'll answer your questions, heal your broken heart, and show you the authority and freedom you can have through my son, Jesus Christ.

It is the power of my love that melts the coldest hearts and fills the most painful voids. Take a deep breath, invite me in, and let's process your disappointments together.

I'm the Source of your existence. I'm here. I always have been and always will be.

With an eternal love,

Abba

Introduction

Being a bastard is a mindset. Actually, it's a lie. It's adapting to a negative way to view one's self based on someone else's definition of you. This word was crafted to make you feel inferior because you were born out of wedlock or you are the offspring of a deadbeat or absent father. Some people use this hurtful language as if a child holds any responsibility surrounding their conception or birth.

Bastard and illegitimate are terminologies used to identify children born to unmarried parents. Some would argue that if something's illegitimate, it has no value, but the very fact that you are alive negates any illegitimacy about you. You are the expressed intent and desire of a loving God. Your heavenly Father has always had plans for your life and He has loved you before your birth. You are not a mistake. You are not an accident.

Your birth was not a surprise to God. It may have been unexpected, unplanned, or even unwanted by your parents, but every child born was divinely allowed. God is the one that gives life, and His intent for you is to be impactful and a gift to this world.

A bastard mindset is one that is self-seeking and can make you feel that if you don't look out for yourself, then who will? This belief will cause you to develop coping mechanisms to camouflage your pain. People who suffer from this debilitating disease often build walls to keep others out or at bay because they don't want to feel the sting of rejection. To have the upper hand, they often subconsciously hurt others to avoid being hurt first. It's the game of let me hurt you before you hurt me, so I can continue to protect the wounds I've so masterfully hidden. What a sad way to go through life.

A father should be a daughter's first love and a son's first hero. A good father is a guiding example for which children learn what acceptable behavior is for men. Unfortunately, this is not always the case. I used to wonder how a man could walk away from something that he helped to create. And often, you internalize it and wonder if you, the child, had anything to do with his leaving or lack of interest in raising or taking care of you. I've come to realize the problem is not with you, it belongs to the parent who willfully walked away.

Let me say that again: The problem is not you. Despite being the one left to deal with the repercussions of a father who chose not to be there for his children, it is still your responsibility to heal. It can feel like an unfair burden, but the very fact that you've been given this obstacle must mean that you have within you the fortitude to overcome it.

I've come to realize that most absent fathers are struggling with their own inabilities, limitations, and unhealed trauma. This doesn't absolve them from their decisions or the pain they caused, but we must recognize that there may be issues that reside within a man who doesn't possess the abilities to be a good father.

By God's design, fathers are supposed to be the protectors and providers of their families. So when a man willingly neglects his role as the foundation he was created to be, it causes a malfunction in the family unit. If the foundation is weak, so will be anything that's built upon it.

This is why being a father is such a great responsibility and a role that should not be taken lightly, because the effects of an absent or absentee dad can bring years of turmoil, anxiety, and years of pain.

INTRODUCTION

We throw the word bastard around all the time, but it's more of a negative mindset than it is a character flaw. It's universal and not just limited to fatherlessness. I've seen the bastard mindset on display in the workplace, social and professional organizations, and even in places of worship.

Self-centeredness is a key indicator of a bastard mindset. It will lead you to have a false belief that getting to the top by any means necessary is acceptable, regardless of who gets hurt along the way. How do you think the term selfish bastard came about? These types of people only look out for their own successes, and it's oftentimes at the expense of others.

You may say, what does that have to do with growing up without a father? Remember, if father means foundation, then any person who is operating with a bastard mindset is functioning with foundational and identity issues.

Our life experiences bleed throughout everything we do; they are incorporated into everything we are. It is undeniable that the things that have happened to you play a part in the way you see yourself, others, and the world. Whether they are good or bad, the residue of your experiences can be seen in your beliefs, choices, and interactions.

If your father was absent, or if he was an absentee father, which means he was present physically but absent emotionally, there are some steps you can take and Biblical principles you can apply to open your heart and reprogram the way you think so peace can reign in your life.

This book was written to share how I was liberated from the bondage of hate and unforgiveness. I'll share with you ways to process the pain, frustration, and disappointments of your father not living up to his role and responsibilities as a dad.

Most importantly, you'll get God's point of view on fatherlessness and His Divine ways to overcome its effects.

If you have questions surrounding your existence, ask God. He has all the answers. One would think that the person who believes in an intentional, omniscient God would find peace in knowing that if He foresaw everything surrounding my life and still allowed me to be born, then there must be a reason. But, honestly, that didn't bring me much comfort.

So, I asked God, "Why?" He said, "I knew what I put in you was greater than the things that would come against you. That's why you need to find your identity in me. I've called you an overcomer, more than a conqueror, an heir, beloved, redeemed, and the list goes on. If you focus on what wasn't instead of what is, you'll miss precious opportunities to really experience the greatness of my power and the depth of my love."

If any of this resonates with you, and you're ready to begin the journey toward healing, let's go!

Chapter 1

Plague of Unforgiveness

Unforgiveness looks like pain camouflaged in happiness, sadness drowned out by laughter, and despair covered with a smile. To the untrained eye, you may not see past the hidden facades to view the real issues lying underneath. Just like camouflage clothing helps you to blend into your surroundings and hide in plain sight, the same is true for those who have mastered the art of hiding their pain. On the other hand, you're probably not masking your pain as well as you think you are.

A plague, by definition, is a disastrous or evil affliction; a cause of irritation or continual trouble or distress. Unforgiveness cannot be compartmentalized. It cannot be isolated, although it is isolating. Some may think that no one can see what they are dealing with internally because a plague can blind you to the deterioration it's causing. However, your invisible scars become highly visible in ways that you may think are unnoticeable. Leaving those around you to wonder, why are you the way you are, or questioning who hurt you? Until unforgiveness is properly dealt with and eradicated, you will have continual battles—no matter where you live, what titles you acquire, or how much money you make.

Unforgiveness is linked to higher incidences of stress, heart disease, high blood pressure, lowered immune response, cancer, anxiety, depression, and other health issues, according to a Johns Hopkins study.[1] Broken relationships affect us deeply, especially when bitterness sets in.

Unforgiveness is gangrene of the soul. If left untreated, a little black spot on a person's toe will eventually cover the entire body, causing the loss of extremities and leaving the person permanently disfigured, affecting their quality of life. Hate in your heart will render the same results. I assure you that until you deal with your pain, you can move anywhere on this beautiful planet and the same issues will arise. If you're emotionally broken in America, you'll still be broken in Dubai. If you move to a new place and take the old you, you're going to have the same problems and be subject to negative repetitive cycles in your relationships.

The saying is true; you may not be able to control what happens to you, but you can control how you react to it. Don't become the perpetrator of your own pain. Think of unforgiveness as a gateway drug. Smoking, drug use, excessive drinking, and overeating are all coping mechanisms and numbing agents for people who refuse to deal with their problems. Many years may have passed since the issue occurred that hurt you, but now you are self-inflicting harm by doing everything else besides finding ways to heal. What do you do when the enemy is the inner you? You have now become the culprit in your own captivity. Therefore, forgiveness shouldn't be predicated on an apology. Don't waste years and give up your power to be free by waiting for someone to say sorry. Forgiveness is a choice, not a feeling. And don't think that just because you're forgiving

---

1 https://www.hopkinsmedicine.org/health/wellness-and-prevention/forgiveness-your-health-depends-on-it

someone, you're disregarding their harmful actions. By forgiving them, you're not only acknowledging the hurt, but you are also stripping it of the power to continue to cause you pain.

Unforgiveness is ugly, and its effects are ruthless. It's a thief that can rob you of all that's beautiful in your life. Not only have I experienced it personally, but I've also gotten to see the effects of unforgiveness displayed in the lives of others.

There's an older lady that was very dear to me. I've seen firsthand how her inability to forgive has polluted her life, leaving behind just a shell of a person. She's lived most of her days numb and merely going day to day with no true peace or joy. She shared with me that she was raised by an abusive stepfather. He was so abusive that she used to sneak out of her room at night and hide in a tree until the morning just so he couldn't find her. Many days, he would threaten to beat her until she was bloodied and often told her he would bash her brains out. Thankfully, she survived that torment, but when she became old enough to marry, she ended up marrying a man who was just like her stepdad. Her husband verbally and physically abused her, too.

Could she have chosen a better spouse? Sure. But maybe her example of love was tainted by what she experienced growing up. Inevitably, if a woman gets married, she will either marry someone like her father, the exact opposite, or someone with the attributes she wished her father had. Those are the three options. That's why it's so important for mothers to choose well and be highly selective about the person with whom they procreate.

This older lady has held on to resentment and hurt for decades; almost all of her life. And slowly but surely, the hate calcified and hardened her heart. She's battled years of drinking, trying to outrun her memories. What I found to be saddest of all is that in her golden years, when she should be reminiscing about her life and accomplishments, she was still burdened by her pain.

Often, she would be lost in the recesses of her mind, replaying the things that had been done to her. She became despondent and wasn't fully engaged in life. There wasn't even an escape for her when she was asleep, because even then, she would be haunted by her dreams. All night she tosses and turns, fights, and screams about the issues she won't release. Forgiving and releasing those who've hurt her could have led to a life of victory; instead, harboring those resentments has only resulted in years wasted away.

Oftentimes, I've wept for her pain-filled days and restless nights.

JOURNAL PROMPT:

What are your coping mechanisms for dealing with pain?

JOURNAL PROMPT:

What are your coping mechanisms for dealing with pain?

Chapter II

Love

I happened to come across a journal I had while in high school. I don't think I realized just how much pain I was in until I read a few of my entries. Because I believe that transparency leads to healing, I'm going to share them with you.

Journal Entry: April 2000

My mind tends to run on my so-called father a lot. When I think about him, I feel so abandoned, as if I did something to deserve to be ignored. I have a pain in my heart that I feel will never go away. I used to be so jealous of my cousins because their fathers were there. It was like I was the only bastard in the family.

I know that my father has been sick, but I can't even call him to see how he's doing because he's never given me his home number. I don't know why he's ashamed of me. I can remember very vividly one day my mom and I went to meet him to get some money. I got out of the car, ran up to give him a hug, and he stopped me in my tracks. Literally, he put his hand on my shoulder to avoid the embrace. And you know his reasoning for doing this? He said I couldn't hug him in public because someone may see him. I was ten when this happened. The innocence of my youth was gone. My world was shattered. This is the day my father broke my heart.

I feel like crap! I did not ask to be born. I cannot control the choices he made. I hate him! I could get the feeling of rejection at school, work, and even from my friends, but I shouldn't be rejected by my father.

I know it's bad to say I hate him; it's just that every time I see him it makes my stomach hurt and I want to puke. He claims me when we are alone, but I've never been to his house for Christmas, Thanksgiving, Easter, New Year's…nothing.

The point is, I've never been to his house with his family. I guess because I am not a part of his family. I don't acknowledge him as my father. He's nothing to me. I thank God for my mommy because she's the only one I have. And I try to do my best to make things easier for her because it is so hard on her being a single mother of a teen.

Sometimes I wonder why I was dealt the hand that I have, but I know God makes no mistakes. I pray He will help me with my anger.

*Written by seventeen-year-old Shaunta.

You combat hate with love. I know, I know that sounds too fairytale-ish, easier said than done, too far fetched. However, like forgiveness, love is not a feeling, it's a choice. When I tell people this simple yet profound truth, it's often met with a scoff and the rebuttal, "but you don't know what they've done to me. I'll never forgive them."

I empathize with you, I really do. But I urge you to not let your hurt turn into hate. This may be a hard lesson to learn because hating someone who has wronged you can be justifiable, but hating only breeds contempt and more hate, which only leads to more pain. It's a never-ending pattern. It took me a long time to realize that by hating my father, I hated a part of myself.

This was clear in some decisions I made, like losing my virginity in my early teens, staying in toxic relationships, and masking my insecurities with a bad attitude. Yours may be people pleasing or the constant need to overachieve. Sometimes when people act unlovable, it's because they are feeling unloved. But even in my professed hatred for my father and his actions, or lack thereof, there was still a longing to be wanted and acknowledged by him.

Every time I thought back on that dreadful day, I could still feel the weight of his hand pushing me away, the sting of the tears welling up in my eyes, and the shame that overcame me with the realization that I was a secret. I allowed this hurt to fester until anger was the only emotion I could express. My world came crashing down. Suddenly, I felt violated, vulnerable, and confused. My foundation was cracking right before my eyes.

I knew my parents had met while my father was separated from his wife. I knew he was a pastor, a bishop, in fact. And I knew where he lived. Supposedly, I was an answered prayer because he and his wife couldn't conceive and he had always wanted a child of his own. I was a daddy's girl in the beginning and we had the best bond. He was my daddy and I was his baby girl.

At first, I was content with the little that I knew. It never dawned on me that public knowledge of my existence would ruin things for him. I thought it was normal for him, my mom, and me to meet almost every

Saturday for breakfast. We would often go to McDonald's or the Shoney's buffet. These meetups would be the highlight of my week. I would sit next to him in the booth, lay my head on his arm, and we would talk about school, books, and Barbies. He always paid for breakfast, and he always gave us money for the week.

As I got older, I realized that we would be meeting across town from where he lived. I guess he was okay with displaying affection for me in places where he thought he wasn't as recognizable.

My dad was a contractor by trade and a lifelong entrepreneur. He built the house I grew up in. It was a beautiful four-bedroom, two-bathroom ranch style home that he said he built as a gift to my mom for having me and giving him the child that he always wanted. This was in 1983, way before push gifts were a thing. It was this same house where I remember he and I would play on the living room floor and read books together all the time.

But, after the 'you can't hug me in public' incident our relationship became strained. I loathed the very person I had once loved so much. The things that never bothered me before started to make my blood boil. I started asking questions about why things were the way they were. Eventually his calls slowed, the visits stopped, and the weekly Saturday breakfast dates became sporadic until they were nonexistent.

I was told that I was his only biological child and that although he wanted to marry my mom, after she found out that he was not divorced, she urged him to work things out with his wife, with whom he had adopted children.

Adopted children? Imagine my shock! The knowledge of that threw me for a loop. Honestly, it left me perplexed. Jealousy started to rise up in my heart. Ah, now I see. His adopted children get the lion's share of him and all that's reserved for me are the scraps. I envied what they had, not the material things, but the access to his time and heart. I couldn't wrap my head around how he was capable of loving and wanting children, but not the one he asked for and helped to create.

As I matured in my walk with Christ, I came to realize that I cannot love God and hate my father. It is im-pos-sible. Even though I desperately wanted to hold him hostage to the pain that he caused, and I felt it was well within my rights to do so, I knew that if I ever wanted to experience God's best, I had to love and forgive my dad. And I'm not just talking empty words like, oh yeah, I love my father. I mean a true conviction that would cause my words to be followed by actions.

Every fiber of my being did not want to do this. He was wrong, not me. I wanted to nurse that hurt and remind him every chance I got. But, deep inside I had an insatiable desire to become all that God had destined for me. I knew that for me to live the great life I know God had planned, I needed to make amends with my father. Moreover, the Bible says, "If someone says, 'I love God,' but hates a fellow believer, that person is a liar; for if we don't love people we can see, how can we love God, whom we cannot see?" (1 John 4:20 NLT). Wait. Say what now? Did God just call me a liar? Yes, that's exactly what he did.

Talk about snatching my edges! Besides having to love my father, I came across the scripture that commanded me to honor him, too. Ephesians 6:1–3 says, "Children, obey your parents in the Lord [that is, accept their guidance and discipline as His representatives], for this is right [for obedience teaches wisdom and self-discipline]. Honor [esteem, value as precious] your father and your mother [and be respectful to them]—this is the first commandment with a promise so that it may be well with you, and that you may have a long life on the earth" (AMP).

So, now I've been called a liar and my life expectancy may decrease by harboring unforgiveness and refusing to honor my dad. I was like, but God, what about the next part of the scripture that tells fathers not to provoke their children to wrath? What about that? Because, certainly, I have been provoked.

I would pray and ask God, "How do I honor someone I don't even like or respect?" Nevertheless, I decided I better figure it out so that I could heal because I was starting to dislike the person I was becoming. It's the job of the devil to take beautiful things and taint them. I didn't want to be tainted any longer, so I prayed for God to take away the hurt, disappointment, and feelings of rejection. You know what I found out? I had to put in some effort as well. Many times we say we're waiting on God, but in reality, he's actually waiting on us to make a move. Your healing is up to you. You have to play a part in your own deliverance. In the book of Hebrews it says, "For the word of God is alive and active. Sharper than any double-edged sword, it penetrates even to dividing soul and spirit, joints and marrow; it judges the thoughts and attitudes of the heart" (Hebrews 4:12 NIV).

If this scripture is true, and the Word of God is alive and active, then reading, reciting, meditating, and acting on it has to produce fruit.

I used 1 Corinthians 13:47 (AMP) as my guide: "Love endures with patience and serenity, love is kind and thoughtful, and is not jealous or envious; love does not brag and is not proud or arrogant. It is not rude; it is not self-seeking, it is not provoked [nor overly sensitive and easily angered]; it does not take into account a wrong endured. It does not rejoice at injustice, but rejoices with the truth [when right and truth prevail]. Love bears all things [regardless of what comes], believes all things [looking for the best in each one], hopes all things [remaining steadfast during difficult times], endures all things [without weakening]."

Spend time in prayer, open your heart, and exchange your negative words and thoughts for positive ones. I used to feel that my father was a coward and took the easy way out by not taking care of his responsibilities, but instead of rehearsing the aspects about him I didn't like, I reinforced my forgiveness toward him with positive declarations. So if I was mad thinking about my father's cowardly acts, I would pray that God will allow him to exercise boldness and strength to confront his actions and do what's right.

Another way to start the healing process toward forgiveness is to insert your name in the scripture above. For example, Shaunta endures with patience and serenity, Shaunta is kind and thoughtful; Shaunta is not jealous or envious. The power of life and death is in what you speak. Whenever a negative thought arises, replace it with one of the attributes of love. Start thinking about your father according to this scripture. When you feel yourself getting angry, be reminded that love is not easily angered and keeps no record of wrong.

Love will make you look for the best in your father, even if he's done you a lifetime of misdeeds. And even if there's no good to be found, love and forgiveness will allow you to make room for yourself to experience the freedom of healing that you deserve.

I often wondered what could cause a father to abandon their children and forfeit the joy of a relationship with them? Regardless of the reasoning, the miracle is that you are here. You're alive and your life has meaning; that within itself is enough to be grateful. Love will help you calm your emotions. No longer will you be subject to swinging from the pendulum of uncertainty. Love will give you the confidence you need to love yourself and others without inhibition or fear of giving love away and not receiving it in return.

This is why love is the first step to finding peace. Remember, I spoke about strong foundations earlier in the book? Well, that's exactly what love is. You start with love and build from there; without it, everything else is in vain. Love is the fountain from which all other benefits flow.

As the poet Maya Angelou so eloquently puts it, "Love recognizes no barriers. It jumps hurdles, leaps fences, penetrates walls to arrive at its destination full of hope." This is the kind of love God has for us; it's limitless and can't be contained. And this is the kind of love we should have for ourselves and each other. Love yourself enough to heal.

JOURNAL PROMPT:

Are there any good memories you have of your dad?

What scriptures can you use to replace negative feelings and thoughts about your father?

JOURNAL PROMPT:

Are there any good memories you have of your dad?

What scriptures can you use to replace negative feelings and thoughts about your father?

Chapter III

Forgive

Journal Entry: July 26, 2000

God is so good. He lets us sin, but then he showers his grace and mercy on us, which allows us to receive forgiveness. I love God so much and I thank him for the opportunity to let me realize my ways and change. It's going to be hard, but that just makes the reward much better because you learn to appreciate things when you work hard for it. I want to be that light that shines brightly for Christ.

God makes no mistakes. It seems as though I'm giving up a lot to do what's right, but I'm gaining much more than I'll ever lose. Jesus didn't have to think twice about giving his life for me, so why should I be dwelling over not being able to go out and party? I thank God for everything, especially my mother. I love her and don't want to disappoint her in any way. It's just that I've been suffering with something in silence.

I know I am not a boy and I'm not supposed to need a male influence in my life, but I wish my father cared about me. Every time I think about him, I feel so alone. It's hard to know that you have a parent in the same state as you, a matter of fact, less than an hour away from you, and they still want nothing to do with you. I know it's wrong, but I've built up hate toward him and that's not Christlike.

Many years ago, I watched the movie *The Scarlet Letter*. It's an adaptation of John Hawthorne's book written in 1850. Set in seventeenth-century Puritan Boston, Massachusetts, it tells the story of Hester Prynne, who conceives a daughter through an affair and struggles to create a new life of repentance and dignity. Throughout the book, Hawthorne explores themes of legalism, sin, and guilt (Wikipedia). The symbolism in this movie resonated with me because I could see the similarities from the 1800s playing out in my life. The scrutiny of the women who bore children out of wedlock is very much the same today as it was centuries ago. People may not verbalize it, but there is an unspoken stigma.

In the movie, I can remember the single mother having to wear a red 'A' on her clothes to identify that she was an adulterer. It always bothered me that the men weren't subjected to the same punishment; as if the woman was solely responsible for the consequences of both of their actions. Maybe they should have read Isaiah 1:18 (AMP), "'Come now, and let us reason together,' says the Lord. 'Though your sins are like scarlet, they shall be as white as snow; though they are red like crimson, they shall be like wool.'"

I always felt I wore the badge of my parents' indiscretions. Although my mom would tell me I was an answered prayer, I must admit, at times, I certainly didn't feel like one. I shared the same last name as my older siblings but never really felt a true connection to their paternal side of the family. No one treated me like one, but I often felt like an outsider.

No child asks to be born. Could this be why God said he would be a father to the fatherless because he knew the disdain, shame, and hardships that awaited those who grow up without a loving father in their lives?

There are benefits to being a born-again believer; our protection and provision come from God, which further proves my point. How can you be a bastard when God Almighty has said he is your father? Although this passage of scripture is specific to Prophet Jeremiah's life, it's applicable to every child of God. "Before I formed you in the womb, I knew you (and approved of you as My chosen instrument), and before you were born, I consecrated you to Myself as My own" (Jeremiah 1:5 AMP).

Through forgiveness, I realized I am not the scarlet letter for which anyone should be ashamed. Nor will I carry the weight for someone else's sin. I will, however, forgive you as I would want my heavenly father to forgive me, realizing that we are all human, fallible, and subject to making mistakes. I will not live my life with insecurities because of someone else's decisions.

You can't quantify pain, and it's not possible to measure the depth of someone's trauma, but what I do know is that forgiveness liberates and removes the shackles from your heart so that you can love and live freely.

It's commendable to never cause the kind of pain your father caused you, but none of us are perfect. We have or will hurt someone and play a role in their pain, whether it is intentional or not.

That's why Matthew 6 is so profound. "For if you forgive others their trespasses [their reckless and willful sins], your heavenly Father will also forgive you. But if you do not forgive others [nurturing your hurt and anger with the result that it interferes with your relationship with God], then your Father will not forgive your trespasses" (Matthew 6:14–15 AMP).

The prerequisite for your forgiveness is based on how well you forgive others.

Pain is inevitable, but suffering is a choice. Shift your motives; don't say you're going to forgive just to prove you're the bigger or better person. Forgive because you desire the emotional intelligence to navigate this life in the best way and the spiritual intelligence to rob the enemy of any ammunition.

Here's how you can do that:

Do an unforgiveness detox. Write down everything you're holding against your father in one column and on the opposite side, write down I forgive you by each one. If you find you can't write I forgive you for certain things, make those issues your prayer points until the day comes when you can honestly say those issues no longer have a hold on you.

For example:

He abandoned me.	
He molested me.	
He abused me.	
He rejected me.	
He never came to any important events in my life.	

If you have your father's number, call him and tell him you've forgiven him for the wrong he's done. It's imperative that you release these words into the atmosphere because just thinking it or convincing yourself that you've forgiven isn't good enough. When you do that, you're really only fooling yourself. God knows your heart and can see in those hidden crevices where unforgiveness may be tucked away.

Be forewarned, releasing these words in the atmosphere will be tested. You may think you're walking in forgiveness until an opportunity to show love arises and your feelings of selfishness or anger resurface.

Lastly, if you have a picture of your father, and it's not triggering deep emotional trauma, place it somewhere you're prone to see it every day. When you see it in passing, be intentional about praying for him. Here are some examples of what you can pray for:

>That God gives him the conviction to do what's right.
>That he'll become a man of great character and choices.
>For his healing.
>For his mental, physical, and financial well-being.
>For the bloodline that God allowed you to be birthed through.
>Pray against generational curses.

If it's your desire, pray for reconciliation and a renewed relationship.

When praying for the cleansing of your bloodline, know that unforgiveness is an open door that allows access to the devil to wreak havoc in your life or the lives of the generations that will follow you. Because the Kingdom of Heaven is a government, it operates by laws and principles. Revelation 12:10 says that Satan accuses God's people night and day. If you want to see consistent breakthroughs in any area of your life or grow in your walk with God, be sure to remain in right standing with Him. Accusations can hold up blessings, bring on sickness and disease, and could even impact your children and their children. It can bring on spiritual attacks and physical setbacks.

As you're doing this, hate, resentment, and hurt will start to melt away. It will not be an overnight process, but the more you do it, the easier it'll become. If light and darkness cannot dwell in the same place, the same must be true for love and hate. If you're releasing words of love for your father, hate has no other choice but to evacuate your heart and mind. Remember, you're not doing this for him, you're doing this for you.

In 2013, I did a 21-day fast. I knew a stronghold had taken root in my heart and was trying to hold me captive to my pain and problems forever. I needed deliverance and I was determined to get it. This was by far the hardest thing I've ever done, but I was committed to the process.

Fasting and prayer are mighty weapons as told by Jesus in Matthew 17:21. Fasting disciplines our flesh and mind and corrects our heart's posture. This is why it's such a valuable weapon for the believer; it breaks strongholds and clears out the debris of the world so we can hear God more clearly, discern His position in a matter, govern our lives according to His word, and increase in power.

You may be the strength that causes your father's deliverance. As you do this, you may find yourself thinking of your father with a smile, or imagining his face and having compassion, or even choosing to believe the good about him with the hopeful belief that if he truly knew better, he would have done better. Could it be that someone failed him along the way? Possibly his own father?

Forgiveness is a weapon.

JOURNAL PROMPT:

Ask Holy Spirit to reveal anyone you owe an apology,

and/or need to forgive.

JOURNAL PROMPT:

Ask Holy Spirit to reveal anyone you owe an apology,

and/or need to forgive.

Chapter IV

Release

Journal Entry: August 27, 2000

Today my heart is a little sad because I constantly think about my father. I think about the fact that he doesn't claim me. If there is something that I've done, please let me know so I may correct my problem. I have no feelings toward him anymore. I wish him the best of health and success. There was once a time when I longed for a relationship with him, but now I couldn't care less about getting to know him. It's kind of hard for someone to tell you they love you and don't show any actions. I don't want his money; all I really want is some of his time. Don't hate me for your sins. I wish I had never met him. I would rather have someone live across the country from me that has never seen me than have you live an hour away and deny my existence. I think he's a hypocrite and a liar. How can you be a servant of God and try to hide the truth at the same time?

I pray every night that God will help me forgive, but I keep thinking, how can you forgive someone who acknowledged no wrongdoing? My mom always wants me to talk about my feelings, but she can't really relate because she had a great father. As a matter of fact, I don't have anyone who I can relate to.

Anyway, God is my father and he will never disown me. He will stand by my side, so whatever I do, I do for Christ. Unlike my father, I am not ashamed of what I am or who I stand for. It's hard that my biological father doesn't want to take an interest in me. If he took the time, he would find out that I'm pretty cool.

As you can see from my journal entries, I was in turmoil, and I severely needed peace. I read a quote that said, "Peace begins with love." Without love, everything is pointless.

I've heard many times that God will give you peace like a river. The significance of this analogy is that just like water, the accumulation and release of peace will cut through any hardened heart or impenetrable force. Over time, a mountain can become a canyon because of the persistence and pressure of the water flowing down it. Peace is the same way. If you allow the peace of God to cover your life, it will sever, erode, and wash away anything that is trying to block your life of abundance.

There's a process to everything. Erosion happens over time; it isn't an overnight process. The same is true for your deliverance from a bastard mindset. It'll take time, patience, and practice. So don't give up on the process if you fall back into your old habits or feel like it isn't working.

Dr. Myles Munroe, a New York Times bestselling author and world-renowned lecturer, stated in one of his teachings that how you got here is not as important as you being here. Don't get caught up with the details surrounding your birth, your conception, or with whom God allowed to be your parents. You're here and that's truly all that matters. And now that you're here, take some time to find out why. Let your pain lead you to your purpose.

A bastard mindset is dangerous because it distorts your outlook on life. It'll make you feel that you're in this world alone and that no one cares. I mean, if your own father walked away, how can you expect or trust anyone else to be honest and dedicated to you? This kind of heartbreak is hard to heal, but just because something is hard doesn't mean it's impossible.

Thinking this way will inevitably bleed into who you are and corrupt the very essence of who you can become. Abandonment or rejection issues will leave you mad at the world, walking around with a chip on your shoulder. If left unattended, that rock will become a boulder, and eventually, that boulder will become a mountain. This mountain can obstruct the beauty in your life and can also be a problem in the lives of others. See, your healing isn't just for you. Other people are depending on you to release this hurt so they can either learn from your life or not be subjected to these issues at all.

The weight of a father's absence or abuse can consume and crush you, leaving behind only remnants of a person. It'll make you afraid to love, afraid to trust, and to a certain extent, afraid to live.

The definition of release means to allow or enable to escape from confinement. Holding onto unforgiveness can literally kill you. You think you have things under control and that you're handling it, but all you're doing is hiding the pain, harboring resentment, and holding onto the hurt. Release all of that once and for all. Otherwise, it'll fester and become cancerous, destroying and stealing the very essence of who you are.

Don't suppress your hurt under the guise of being strong, because the façade of your confidence will one day be challenged. A lot of fatherless girls and women tend to exude sexuality and become hypersexualized, but all they truly want is to be loved. If the saying is true, bad press is better than no press, fatherless daughters tend to feel that any attention is better than no attention.

A few years ago, I came across an article by researchers at Vanderbilt University, Nashville, Tennessee. I was researching if there was any scientific explanation or correlation of high rates of promiscuity in fatherless girls. According to the research,[2] "A young girl's relationship with her family, especially with her father, may influence at what age she enters puberty." The study examined 173 girls and their families from Nashville and Knoxville, Tennessee, and Bloomington, Indiana, from the time the girls were in pre-kindergarten until they were in the seventh grade.

"Those who had close, positive relationships with their parents during the first five years of life tended to experience relatively late puberty, compared to girls who had more distant relationships. More specifically, it was found that the quality of fathers' involvement with daughters was the most important feature of the early family environment in relation to the timing of the daughters' puberty."

"Girls who are raised in father-absent homes or dysfunctional father-present homes experienced relatively early pubertal timing. One biological explanation is that girls whose fathers are not present in the home may be exposed to other adult males—stepfathers or their mothers' boyfriends—and that exposure to pheromones (chemical substances that exude an aroma which is a sexual stimulant) produced by unrelated adult males accelerates female pubertal development. The flip side of that theory is that a girl who lives with her biological father in a positive environment

---

[2] https://www.sciencedaily.com/releases/1999/09/990927064822.htm

is exposed to his pheromones and is inhibited from puberty, perhaps as a natural incest avoidance mechanism. Girls who live with their fathers, but have a cold or distant relationship with them, would not be exposed to their fathers' pheromones as much as those who have more interaction, therefore causing daughters in the distant relationship to reach puberty earlier" (Father-Daughter Relationship is Crucial from the Society for the Advancement of Education).

In my summation of the study, I realized that there's a chemical component in fathers that offsets puberty, causing a girl's body to react differently when her father is not a part of her life. This can open the door to seeking attention, affection, and having intimate desires for men when in reality, all your body is really missing is the love and presence of a good father.

Ladies, have you ever worked with another woman for so long, or lived with other females, and you one day realized that your monthly cycle had synced with theirs, and you all started getting your periods around the same time? It's all hormonal because there's a chemical reaction at play. Some of us during that time of the month would experience PMS—Premenstrual Syndrome. These triggers are an indicator that you may start your monthly cycle soon. You may experience mood swings, cramping, bloating, headaches, fever, chills, etc. And symptoms vary in degree and length of discomfort based on the individual.

Well, what if I told you that acting out, promiscuity, low self-esteem, anger, resentment, or any other self-destructive behavior was because some girls and women are experiencing DMS—Daddy's Missing Syndrome.

There's a physical and chemical reaction that takes place in girls when their father is absent. Just like when your brain tells you to eat and drink when you're hungry and thirsty, your brain also tells you to seek male companionship to fill the void of the essential missing man in your life. Your brain is the most powerful part of your body. If you can change your mind, you can change your life.

Symptoms of DMS can be mild or severe and can last for days or your entire life. The family unit was God's idea. He created it perfectly. God's family consists of a mother, father, and offspring. When we alter God's design, we get adverse results.

Unlike with PMS, you can't truly control your symptoms, but with DMS, you possess all the power to overcome this debilitating and chronic ailment. Inherently, how long you suffer is up to you. I've found that boys and men are often silent sufferers of DMS. While women often display their emotions on their sleeves, men tend to keep their hurt buried deep.

Men will often suffer in silence when dealing with this. Some exude a strong awareness of self, overconfidence, and cockiness, but that could also be a false sense of bravado to hide their emotional trauma.

If you are the product of a childhood that was lacking affection, especially from your father, can you imagine how hard it may be to recognize, reciprocate, and express love? In most cases, it may be true that absentee fathers provide financially, but if he's never articulated his love for you, that can be just as bad as if he wasn't in the home at all.

Some men have never felt the loving embrace of their fathers. In addition, there are some men who've never heard, "Good job, son. I'm proud of you." This presents a dichotomy. On one hand, you have a man who wants to show and express love, but because there was no example, he doesn't know how. Fellas, think back on it. Who did the job your father should have done? Who showed you how to treat a woman? Was it someone in the neighborhood, lyrics from a song, or scenes from a movie or TV show?

It's not rare for fatherless men not to trust other men, or to be emotionally stunted, void of the ability to be vulnerable. Subscribing to the logic that showing emotions is a sign of weakness, they often struggle with feelings of inadequacy and isolation. Something could be really hurting them and causing a great deal of pain, and instead of willingly sharing their feelings, it takes prying with the jaws of life to get them to open up. Women, you may get frustrated, wondering why won't he talk to you, and little do you know; he's struggling with trying to figure out how.

Because daddy was gone, men tend to have commitment issues and women tend to have trust issues. Dating a girl with trust issues is like having four full-time jobs. Trust me, I know, I used to be one of them. Value yourself enough to recognize your shortcomings and then work on them.

The effects of fatherlessness can be long-standing and often generational until someone decides to break the curse. You have to make this decision so your children won't suffer. Slay this giant. If not for you, do it for those that will come after you. You can't choose your parents, but you can choose with whom you parent.

If you're ever going to experience true freedom, you're going to have to release your father from the bondage of what you wanted him to be. We've all heard the saying, you can't control what happens to you, but you can control how you react to it. Don't repay hate with hate. Extend grace so that your life can be beautiful and fragrant with love.

The question may arise: What is there to release? You may tell yourself that you're not holding anyone captive, but that's not true. If when a thought of your father arises, and along with it comes feelings of hurt, pain, and anger, that is an indication that you haven't released him for what he did or did not do for you.

This definition of trauma says it all.

Trauma

"Trauma is a wound that hardens you psychologically that then interferes with your ability to grow and develop. It pains you and now you're acting out of pain. It induces fear and now you're acting out of fear. Trauma is not what happens to you, it's what happens inside you as a result of what happened to you."

Dr. Gabor Maté, renowned expert on trauma, addiction, stress and childhood development

I found this scripture particularly helpful because releasing my dad was the hardest part for me. "Let all bitterness and wrath and anger and clamor [perpetual animosity, resentment, strife, fault-finding] and slander be put away from you, along with every kind of malice [all spitefulness, verbal abuse, malevolence]. Be kind and helpful to one another, tender-hearted [compassionate, understanding], forgiving one another [readily and freely], just as God in Christ also forgave you" (Ephesians 4:31–32 AMP).

What stood out to me the most was that the responsibility fell on me to put away bitterness, anger, and wrath. The proverbial ball was in my court. My healing became a direct correlation to how badly I wanted it. It was no longer dependent upon whether my father acknowledged his wrongdoing. I had the power to release myself from the chains of unforgiveness. I had to forgive my father for not understanding the magnitude of his absence. I had to become responsible enough to take part in my healing. I had to end the cycle; if not, I would have perpetuated this pain unto my children. And though it would have made it easier to love, forgive, and release him if he had admitted to the pain he caused, I realized that his permission, acknowledgment, or repentance was not needed for me to be free.

Once you make a conscious decision that you want to be free and then implement the appropriate steps to achieving that freedom, no person or unjust act can stand in your way. Once you see yourself differently, you'll start changing your habits, speech, and mindset, which, in return, will give you a better life.

If you choose to reach out to your father, I urge you to not push for a particular outcome. Be open to allowing God to work things out His way and in His time. Things happen beautifully when you let God handle it. Your father may not be receptive, but his reaction doesn't stop your healing. At some point, if you want to be free, you're going to have to let go. You cannot change your father, but after applying these steps, you'll realize that you're the one who's changed. If you say you can't do this, remember, you can do all things through Christ who strengthens you (Philippians 4:13).

Stop waiting for your father to show up or change his ways; that may never happen. Loving him is for you. Forgiving him is for you. Releasing him is for you. Now, yes, he may reap the benefits of you doing these things, but he is not the main benefactor; you are.

For many years, I thought God had ignored my prayers and tears from the strained relationship I had with my biological father. And I was angry that I may never know the feeling of a father's love, but boy was I wrong. When I was twenty years old, my mom married a wonderful man who gave selflessly and loved unconditionally. My bonus dad, Will, was the epitome of a father. Not only did he love her, but he loved her children as well. And as an adult, I got to experience what I was missing.

I also got a front-row seat to witness how a man should protect and provide for his family. I credit Will's great example for helping me to recognize those same great attributes in the man I chose to marry. These teachable moments are what a father is supposed to do. This showed me that God's word is true. He answered my prayers, even though it wasn't in the way I was expecting. Forgiveness opens you up to blessings you aren't even aware are awaiting you.

My bonus dad promised to walk me down the aisle to marry the love of my life, and he did just that. Despite being sick and battling cancer, he was there for my wedding day. And as we took steps toward my future husband, I was also walking away from the pains of my past. As Will was fulfilling his promise and fatherly duties to me on that day, the hurt of never seeing my biological father at award ceremonies, graduations, birthdays, or even taking an active part in my life went away.

Six months after my wedding, Will passed away.

I've come to realize that my biological father is not a bad person. He's flawed, just like any of us. He just refused to do anything about his shortcomings. I've traded my hatred for compassion and I no longer hold him accountable for his actions. I'm not his judge. God is.

Hold space for grace. I understand if you're not quite at the point to extend it to your father at this moment, but I implore you to please hold space for it.

Hold space for change, for growth, for forgiveness. It's a wonder what God can do with just a little room.

RELEASE

In 2016, I was compelled to send my biological father a card because I wanted him to know that I was no longer angry with him. I wanted him to experience the freedom that I was enjoying. And a part of me hoped we could reconcile and make efforts to have a healthy relationship, especially now that I have children and wanted them to know their grandfather.

My graduation cards and wedding invitation never received a response, but I was hopeful this time. I pushed past the memory of me showing him my high school graduation pictures and him telling me to give him the smallest one so he could keep it close to him, but I really knew it was because he had to hide it somewhere.

For a while, I tried to write a letter to him, expressing how I felt, and the words just wouldn't come. One day, I was in the store and purchased a 'thinking of you' card. All I felt led to put in it were the following words: I love you. I forgive you. I release you. I enclosed a picture of me and my children, holding a picture of him.

I was trying to build a bridge of redemption, one that I hoped he would be willing to cross. I wanted public acceptance from my father, I wanted to tell him I forgave him for the hurtful things he did, but I also wanted to apologize for things I said. I wanted to feel his embrace.

Unfortunately, we never got a chance to reconcile in person. Just two weeks after sending my father the card, I received a phone call telling me he had unexpectedly passed away. Despite the shocking news, deep down in my heart, I believe he received my card and I pray it brought him peace and freedom.

As I paid my final respects to him, I was overcome with so many emotions. But the strongest of them all was gratitude. It was hard to witness people celebrate a version of my father that I didn't get to experience. However, I am grateful for his life and the part he played in my existence. As I reflect, I've concluded that I'd rather live with the truth than die from pride. I'm not too proud to say that growing up without him was hard, but his absence strengthened and helped me to become a witness to God's grace.

It's been three decades since that fateful day when my father stopped me in my tracks, and there have been a lot of hard lessons I've had to learn because I didn't start this healing process until I was much older. My advice to you is don't waste precious time like I did. Looking back on my life, I can see how God was always there and how he placed special people in my life to remind me of His love.

When God says, He'll never leave or forsake you, that's exactly what He means. Although you may not be cognizant of all the ways He shows that He's there, rest assured that you have a promise from a God who does not lie.

RELEASE

JOURNAL PROMPT:

Can you recognize any trauma traits in your life?

JOURNAL PROMPT:

Can you recognize any trauma traits in your life?

Chapter V

Good Grief

We know good grief is a figure of speech, one that I'm sure I yelled out in frustration a time or two during this season of learning the liberating power of forgiveness. But do you know that it can also be a method to process traumatic experiences? I have experienced both goodness and grief in a way that I never had before. I'm sure you're asking, what could possibly be good about grief? What I've come to realize is that even though we can't redefine certain situations in our lives, we can repurpose them.

I have a spiritual mentor who always seems to call at the right time to encourage me or to share a prophetic message from God concerning my life. She told me that rejection is a tool that drives many toward their destiny. That very statement changed my outlook on life and my situation. I was starting to develop a woe is me mentality; hardships have a way of doing that. The blessing is that there are times when you aren't even praying for yourself, God causes others to pray for you. He loves you just that much.

If you were to ask any of my friends from high school or college, there were two things I always spoke about: the first was moving to New York and the next one was to marry someone rich. Well, in 2010 I moved from South Carolina to New York, and I can truly say my metamorphosis began during this time. I'm eternally grateful for my aunt and uncle, who not only gave me a place to live but space to grow.

This is when I met my former pastor, Bishop Michael Talbert, and his sweet wife, who would later become my uncle and aunt through marriage. God has a way of strategically placing people in our lives who will help catapult our growth. Bishop's biblical teachings were integral in helping me evolve.

Well, isn't this fantastic, I thought, as I rolled my eyes. God would use a preacher to help in my deliverance when it was a preacher who hurt me, but there are no coincidences with the Divine.

It can be especially disheartening when those in power abuse their privilege; we all know it happens way too often. I'm sure a lot of people would develop a disdain for clergy and what they represent because of the actions of a few, but God doesn't want you to adopt this mindset. After someone jeopardizes your trust, it can be easy to become hardened and dismissive.

As a woman, I felt like I was losing my tenderness and succumbing to my desire to be my own savior. But if you read Proverbs 3:5–12, specifically in the Message translation, I'm sure it'll bring you the illumination you need to know that you can never go wrong when you put your trust in God:

> "Trust God from the bottom of your heart;
> don't try to figure out everything on your own.
> Listen for God's voice in everything you do, everywhere you go;

He's the one who will keep you on track.
Don't assume that you know it all.
Run to God! Run from evil!
Your body will glow with health,
your very bones will vibrate with life!
Honor God with everything you own;
give him the first and the best.
Your barns will burst,
your wine vats will brim over.
But don't, dear friend, resent God's discipline;
don't sulk under his loving correction.
It's the child he loves that God corrects;
a father's delight is behind all this."

Ask God to make scripture come alive for you. They're more than just words on paper or accounts of old stories from long ago. When applied, it possesses the power to help change your life.

Bishop Talbert taught with such fervor and conviction that I couldn't resist tuning in to see how I could apply scriptural truths to my life. It became impossible to ignore the pain. I wanted to be free from the prison of unforgiveness, and I realized the only person I could change was me.

Bishop was the first person I heard say, "It doesn't matter what your mother or father did, you're here, and that's enough to be grateful for." One year he made me call and wish my dad a Happy Father's Day. I didn't want to, but I did. To my surprise, he answered and we chatted for a while. As time passed, I would try to check in from time to time, and his number was no longer in service. I guess he changed it. We never spoke again after that day.

I was jaded and didn't forgive my father overnight, but the journey to my liberation had begun. I have a great support system and I encourage you to get one too. Surround yourself with people who aren't afraid to lovingly tell you the truth.

Another thing, you must give your pain a point of expiration. This isn't some arbitrary date on the calendar as much as it's an awareness that you want to have that keeps you moving forward and processing your emotions. Some things you have to leave at the feet of Jesus, knowing that He's capable of helping you navigate and overcome obstacles you never thought you could. Cast all your cares upon Him b/c He cares for you.

When my mom passed, it wrecked my world; I had seen her survive so much. I started to feel like nothing made sense anymore, especially my faith. One day I collapsed on the floor, and the Holy Spirit gently said, "You can mourn with a happy heart." I responded, "I don't know how to do that." Holy Spirit gently whispered, "I'll help you." I compare this type of grieving to a baby learning to walk. You may stumble and fall down, but please try again and get back up and know that there's always help available.

Don't continue to suffer by holding grudges against those who've mistreated you. This is what I know to be true; God will give you an allotted amount of time and opportunities to right your wrongs and also to forgive those who've hurt you, but He won't make you do it. The choice is up to you. You hold the power to no longer live in the captivity of a bastard mentality.

Remember the spiritual mentor I spoke of earlier in this chapter and the caliber of man I claimed I was going to marry? Well, one day, while living in New York, my mentor came to visit and said that God showed her who my husband would be. I wasn't dating at the time, so this took me by surprise. She said that he would be a man of great stature and wealth and one who loved God.

She asked me with her thick Jamaican accent, "Shaunta, what do you have to compliment a man like that?" At first, I laughed her off and said, "All of this," while pointing to myself from head to toe. "I'm a ten all day, and any man would find me to be a wise choice and a beautiful asset to his life."

Needless to say, she was not amused. As she sucked her teeth in the way that only Caribbeans can, she replied, "Sweetheart, yes, you're smart and pretty, but what else?" A man like that is going to need a healed and whole woman who will be able to help him achieve the magnitude of his calling. God wants to do something astounding through the both of you."

After meeting my future husband a few months after this encounter with my mentor, I realized that his assets weren't specifically tied to his physical possessions or financial profits, but they were the dreams and ambitions that God had given him. His desire to impact lives far outweighed his pursuit of money.

However, God has mantled and chosen us for the type of life that reflects His endless resources and inexhaustible power. We've been called to be the light that shows the world that wealth through Christ is attainable.

And we're doing it with a God-given idea. One that's going to revolutionize industries, create new markets, and shift the trajectory of generations to come.

The concept for the invention and business didn't come to my husband until our fourth year of marriage, and I'm grateful that God waited until our union to reveal it to him.

We know, "The man who finds a wife finds a treasure, and he receives favor from the LORD" (Proverbs 18:22 NLT). Once we entered the covenant of a God-ordained marriage, the ideas, strategies, blessings, and opportunities continuously flowed. That certainly sounds like favor to me.

If marrying rich was the only goal, I could've ended up in a trophy wife, shut up and look cute type of situation. And if you know me, you know that wouldn't have ended well.

But as my mama would say, "A hint to the wise is sufficient." As a wife, it's good to know the power of your position. We are the conduits through which God uses to unlock the best in any situation. We add value in every way, and by God's design, we are the secret weapon that galvanizes greatness.

Submitting to a man who's submitted to God brings so much pleasure and peace. Listen, I'll follow my husband anywhere and support him in anything because I know he is submitted to and follows God.

It's an honor to be with a man who's committed to being who God called him to be. Not just for our own personal gain but for the world.

I'm reminded of this scripture: "And you shall remember the LORD your God, for it is He who gives you power to get wealth, that He may establish His covenant which He swore to your fathers, as it is this day" (Deuteronomy 8:18 NKJV).

Had I not released the anger, pain, and resentment I was harboring, I would not have been capable of becoming the woman, wife, and mother that God desired for me to be.

So, choose today to love, forgive, and release. Perpetually do this and I guarantee you'll start to see all the beauty life has to offer. This kind of beauty doesn't come from the exterior physical aesthetics of an artificially curated life, but it comes from being renewed.

JOURNAL PROMPT:

Write down your good grief moments and how you've navigated them.

JOURNAL PROMPT:

Write down your good grief moments and how you've navigated them.

Chapter VI

Driving Force

Every report card I've received would say that I was a good student but talked excessively. Literally, every- single-one, from preschool to high school graduation. However, I vividly remember when I was in the fifth grade, our class was given an assignment to write a letter to our parents telling them what we wanted to be when we grew up. I remember writing this note to my mom, letting her know that one day, just like Oprah, my mouth was going to make me rich. I've always had the gift of gab and pride myself on being a good communicator. I naturally thought a career in TV was the path destined for me.

When I went to college, I got my degree in mass communications and broadcasting. I eventually got a job at a news station in the town where my father lived. Now that I reflect on it, that was a strategic move, because I was determined to make him see me. I started out in production, but that wasn't good enough; I wanted to be on the air and have my father turn on the TV to see how great I was doing. And then, he'd feel sorry for not being in my life. My motives for success were wrong. Subconsciously, I was trying to get back at him and show him the error of his ways by proving to him I didn't need him and that I turned out just fine without him. I've heard a lot of celebrities and athletes say that this was their fuel for making millions.

Yup, I, too, had that proverbial chip on my shoulder, something to prove. This chip played out in many of my failed relationships prior to marriage. I became manipulative and demanding; things always had to be my way. I had little to no regard or space to focus on anyone else but myself. I had an 'it's all about me' attitude, not truly caring about anyone else's feelings as long as I got what I wanted. And if you had a problem with that, well, that was, indeed, your problem, not mine.

You see how the bastard mindset was in full effect? My father was primarily the one on the receiving end of these tactics. During college when I needed something or some money, I'd simply call and ask him. But my disposition was he better not tell me no. I'll show up at his church on Sunday and sit in the front row. If I'm being honest, I threatened him with that notion more times than I'm proud to admit.

My dad got me my first car. It was a 1998 black Chevrolet Malibu. It was customized with mirror tint, rims, a banging sound system, airbrushed seats; I mean, the works. It was a cool car and I would get so many compliments on it. I loved that car. All of my friends loved that car.

Proudly I would say, my daddy got it for me. That is, until I found out its origins.

I initially wanted him to buy me a new car, but he told me that he had found one from a friend and he thought I'd really like it. Well, come to find out, the car once belonged to his adopted son and my dad passed it down to me. I assume his son got something better and I got the leftovers.

When I became aware of this, it made me angry. My bastard mindset started kicking in, and instead of being grateful, I became resentful of what I perceived to be a used hand-me-down. A distorted perspective goes hand-in-hand with warped thinking and irrational emotions.

Little did I know, at the time, because the car was custom, it would become a unique identifier.

When I became honest with myself, I realized that my desire to be on TV was tied to my wanting to impress my father, hoping he would then acknowledge me. But here's the problem that comes with trying to impress people; you'll end up doing things solely for recognition. There's a difference between wanting to impress someone and wanting to make someone proud. There's a spirit of competition in trying to impress people versus a spirit of honor that's shared by you and those who are happy for your achievements and because you did your best.

To get to the news station, I would often take the route past my dad's house. So many times, I wanted to pull into the driveway and ring his doorbell and yell, "Surprise" (Cue the song, Jennifer Holliday's "And I Am Telling You"). But I never did. At the back of my mind was always the memory of the time he pushed me away, and I wouldn't dare want to relive that rejection again. I didn't know if he would offer me a warm embrace, call the cops, or drag me off his porch like Mister did Celie and Nettie in the movie *The Color Purple*.

Deep down, we all want to be wanted. I eventually stopped going that way. I didn't want to have to beg for his attention or force him to love me. I especially didn't want to end up on the news or in jail for trespassing. Just because I worked at a news station didn't mean I wanted to be the topic of a segment.

Here's another step to forgiveness: Mourn your loss. As I got older, I realized I needed to mourn the loss of my relationship with my father, and this was well before he passed away. As I processed the feelings associated with grief, it allowed me to move forward. Also, it is quite cathartic to release emotions. Stop keeping things bottled up all the time and take control of your feelings. Some would say to just get over it, but whatever issues you don't deal with, they will eventually present themselves disguised in other areas, and that could be problematic. So don't beat yourself. Cry it out, write out, talk it out.

When someone is "just acting out,' what you're seeing is the fruit of their pain. There's always a root cause for why people think and act a certain way. The experiences in your childhood shape a lot of the person you will become.

An article on WebMD,[3] which was medically reviewed by Dr. Smitha Bhandari, list the stages of grief as:

- Denial: When you first learn of a loss, it's normal to think, "This isn't happening." You may feel shocked or numb. This is a temporary way to deal with the rush of overwhelming emotion. It's a defense mechanism.

- Anger: As reality sets in, you're faced with the pain of your loss. You may feel frustrated and helpless. These feelings later turn into anger. You might direct it toward other people, a higher power, or life in general. To be angry with a loved one who died and left you alone is natural, too.

- Bargaining: During this stage, you dwell on what you could've done to prevent the loss. Common thoughts are "If only…" and "What if…" You may also try to strike a deal with a higher power.

---

3 https://www.webmd.com/depression/depression-grief

- Depression: Sadness sets in as you begin to understand the loss and its effect on your life. Signs of depression include crying, sleep issues, and a decreased appetite. You may feel overwhelmed, regretful, and lonely.

- Acceptance: In this final stage of grief, you accept the reality of your loss. It can't be changed. Although you still feel sad, you're able to start moving forward with your life.

Have you experienced any or all of these stages? If so, write them down and process the effects it has had on you. The voyage between denial and acceptance can be a winding road, but if you're committed to working through the twists and turns they bring, you'll emerge on the other side better than you were before.

After doing this, mourn and move on. Bury it and be done. Stop rehearsing your hurt and rehashing the details that led to your brokenness. Instead, tell your story from a place of victory because you survived. We are all beautifully authored books waiting to be revealed. Having an absent or absentee father is just one chapter in your book; it's not the whole story. So, be encouraged because your experiences may save someone's life or help them through their struggles.

I, too, had to do this. I realized that I was truly healed when my memories no longer carried sorrow with them. I'm able to look back on situations in my life without the pangs of pain. I can recall a story or an encounter and not break down when sharing it. Forgiveness doesn't erase what happened, it empowers you.

Let me say this: Fathers, stop lying to your kids. Don't have them waiting in the window, looking at each passing car, because you told them you were coming and then you don't show up. Most kids already internalize your absence as their fault. Just as the Bible has instructions for how children should revere parents, there's also guidance for how parents should treat their kids. Read Colossians 3:21- AMP. "Fathers, do not provoke or irritate or exasperate your children [with demands that are trivial or unreasonable or humiliating or abusive; nor by favoritism or indifference; treat them tenderly with lovingkindness], so they will not lose heart and become discouraged or unmotivated [with their spirits broken]."

Wow! A father has a direct correlation to the brokenness of a child's spirit. I wonder if more dads knew this, would they then make better or different choices? I'm sure some of them are probably dealing with their own broken spirits from their daddy issues and by default, only know how to perpetuate the cycle instead of eliminating it. I'm not saying you have to be perfect, but you certainly can be honest. You don't have to live in the home with your child(ren) to be an involved parent.

We all need to be cognizant of how we treat each other because Psalm 127:3 says, "Behold, children are a heritage and gift from the Lord. The fruit of the womb is a reward." This doesn't only apply to newborns. Everyone born has been a child and came through a womb, so we are all gifts from the Lord. We should treat one another accordingly.

One day I was counseling a young girl who was getting in trouble at school. She had recently run away from home, and she and her mother had a very strained relationship. You will find that most fatherless children often have issues with authority. While I was getting to know her story, I couldn't help but identify the fruits of fatherlessness in her actions and words. I asked how her relationship was with her dad. These are her exact words, "Oh, it's good. He's a cellphone daddy." That was a new term, but it made me chuckle a little as I remembered the not-so-pleasant nickname I had coined for my father, too. I used to call him my drive-thru daddy since we met at McDonald's so much.

I thought maybe her dad was in prison and that was his only means of communication, but the reality was quite contrary. He lived around the corner from this young lady and her mother, but she barely sees him, but says she can call him anytime if she needs anything. This is a prime example of what absentee fatherhood looks like. Children know when they are not a priority. Could it possibly be that her acting out in school is a cry for help, attention, love, and affection? Look at me. Notice me. I'm hurting. Does anyone even care? These thoughts are often the silent cries of the misfits and troublemakers.

JOURNAL PROMPT:

Have you ever done anything crazy for attention?

Chapter VII

Lost Childhood

There's an extreme amount of pressure that a fatherless child feels to fill the shoes vacated by a dad that's gone or by one who was never there to begin with. At an all too alarming rate, prepubescent boys have to become the 'man' of the house well before they have even crossed the threshold of becoming a man physically or mentally. And daughters often end up being their mother's shoulder to cry on or a consolatory ear.

What should be a carefree time for a child, filled with imagination and playfulness, is now encumbered with the baggage of life. Children are dealing with adult situations and are growing up way too fast. Parents should protect the innocence of childhood. Sometimes kids are carrying the burdens of adults, having to become the caretaker for their siblings or helping to provide because a one-income household isn't enough to get by. I agree with Frederick Douglass, who said, "It is easier to build strong children than to repair broken men."

When I was younger, I would always get compliments that I was very mature for my age. Well, to be honest, I kind of had no choice. I remember when my mom was diagnosed with breast cancer in 1992. I was only 9 years old. The doctors gave her just a few weeks to live and asked her if she would rather pass away in the hospital or at home because there wasn't anything else they could do. She thanked them for doing all they could and told them to let her go home. My mother boldly said, "Send me home. I am not going to die. God is going to heal me."

Even in her weakened physical state, she said it confidently and emphatically. This statement alone shaped me as a child. The reassurance that I could face situations I felt were going to take me out, but knew that if I cried out to God He would save me.

When the pain of my past became too much to handle. I would often say, "I'm not going to let this kill me. God is going to heal me." You have to say and know this too. Take a few moments right now and scream it at the top of your lungs. "I WILL NOT DIE. GOD IS GOING TO HEAL ME." Life and death are in the power of the tongue, so whatever you speak, you will eventually see.

I was just a child, but I remember being the one to give my mom her first bath when she got home because no one else was there. She'd wake me up in the middle of the night, yelling my name because she was in so much pain and needed me to rub her body down to relieve the discomfort. On days like that, I wished I had an engaged daddy at home that I could talk to or help relieve the responsibility that I had to bear. I longed to sit on his lap and for him to tell me everything would be okay. As my world was crumbling around me, I wondered if he even cared. I couldn't help but wonder, Daddy, where were you when I needed you?

Perspective is everything. I thought my dad was living the high life while I was experiencing deep dark valleys. Seeing him in his silver Mercedes Benz made me think that while my mom and I were struggling to make ends meet, he was living the good life. Everything isn't always what it appears. My dad was suffering, too. But as a child, you're often blinded by your own imagination.

I started getting in trouble in school, being disrespectful to the teacher, and disrupting class. This was a drastic change from my normal behavior; generally, I was an attentive student. So you should be careful what labels you allow people to put on you. If we start addressing the source of an issue, the symptoms will subside. What others called being 'bad' was really my plea for help.

Don't just think a wayward child is hopeless. Do some digging to see what brought about these new, troubling ways. I couldn't really articulate what was really going on, but I remember uncontrollably crying during lunch. When my two friends asked what was wrong, all I could say was, you won't understand because you have a dad at home. Now mind you, as a child, I equated having a dad present as a good thing, not even knowing what kind of dads they had. Theirs could've been abusive or negligent.

As we know, carrying stress is both physically tiring and emotionally exhausting at any age. However, I believe the effects of it are compounded when you're younger. It can make one irrational and irritable.

And while I'm at it, it's a disservice and can be emotionally damaging to place the pressure of 'man of the house' on young boys in the case of their fathers' absences. It's unhealthy and unfair. How do you expect him to positively imitate what he has no example of? Kids need a safe space to be young and carefree.

As the adage goes, hindsight is 20/20 because, as I look back on my childhood, I can see how such a challenging experience helped to cultivate my faith and belief in God. If you subscribe to being an optimist and believe that every cloud has a silver lining, reminisce for just a bit, recollecting your past and chronicling any good memories that may have come about through your adversity.

JOURNAL PROMPT:

Are there any benefits you can attribute to difficulties you've faced?

Chapter VIII

No More

I was afforded the opportunity to speak with a young girl who was exhibiting self-destructive behavior. As we chatted, she told me she was proud that she had waited until she turned thirteen to lose her virginity and that she had already had three sexual partners. This alarmed me, but what shook me even more was what followed. She said her mother called her a slut, and this precious girl could not understand why her mom felt that way. She went on to let me know that she could have had sex when she was ten but decided to wait and her mother should be proud of her for that.

There goes another childhood tainted. Another girl was so willing to give up her treasure because she was never taught its value. This is the case with many girls with absent or uninvolved fathers.

Here are some fatherless stats:

1. Daughters of single parents without a father involved are 53% more likely to marry as teenagers, 711% more likely to have children as teenagers, 164% more likely to have a pre-marital birth, and 92% more likely to get divorced themselves.

2. Adolescent girls raised in a two-parent home with involved fathers are significantly less likely to be sexually active than girls raised without involved fathers.

3. In 2011, children living in female-headed homes with no spouse present had a poverty rate of 47.6%. This is over four times the rate for children living in married-couple families.

4. A study of 263 thirteen to eighteen-year-old adolescent women seeking psychological services found that the adolescents from father-absent homes were 3.5 times more likely to experience pregnancy than were adolescents from father-present homes. Moreover, the rate of pregnancy among adolescents from father-absent homes was 17.4% compared to a four (4) percent rate in the general adolescent population.

5. Disengaged and remote interactions of fathers with infants are a predictor of early behavior problems in children and can lead to externalizing behaviors in children as early as age 1.

6. Children with negative attitudes about school and their teachers experienced avoidance and ambivalence with their fathers. On the other hand, children with a secure attachment to their father and whose father was involved had a higher academic self-concept. The father-child attachment was more associated with the child's social-emotional school outcomes than their academic achievement.

*Information from The Fatherless Generation Foundation and FatherhoodFactor.com, "Fatherless Statistics for the United States | Fatherhood Factor."

We have the power to say 'no more' and change these statistics for the better for the next generation.

If you're lost and feel like your life needs some direction, don't be afraid to ask God what you should do. You don't have to experiment, living your life by trial and error. You can go straight to the source and find out what His plans are for your life.

You may find this scripture helpful; "'For I know the plans and thoughts that I have for you,' says the Lord, 'plans for peace and well-being and not for disaster to give you a future and a hope'" (Jeremiah 29:11 AMP).

Don't let the cause of your father's absence be your issue. Whether it was voluntary, involuntary, or systemic oppression. You still can overcome the effects of his absence.

Reading the above statistics can be disheartening, but the power is within you to choose a different outcome. Here is an exercise I call Harnessing the Power of No More.

Make a list of things that will no longer have a hold over you, and then, on the other side of the column, write ways you can overcome them. It could be prayer, fasting, therapy, gaining more education on a matter, confronting self-sabotaging mindsets, repositioning people, affirmations, etc.

To what things are you going to say, aht-aht, I'm not doing this anymore?

Here are a few to get you started:

Harnessing the Power of No More
No more settling for a life that is inferior to your dreams.
No more letting societal labels determine your worth.
No more procrastination.
No more self-doubt.

JOURNAL PROMPT:

What are you going to say no more to?

JOURNAL PROMPT:

What are you going to say no more to?

Chapter IX

Healed to Heal

Be careful about putting pressure on others to fill the void your father left. Sometimes I'm having a challenging day or I'll be moody and take it out on my husband, but thank God I married someone who doesn't mind telling me the truth. He's quick to ask, "What's the source of your frustration? When he does this, it immediately prompts me to get to the root of the issues causing my displeasure.

My husband and I both grew up fatherless. While we were dating, there were hurdles we had to overcome and habits that needed to change if we were going to be together. Some days we would just drive around town with the top down on his convertible, listening to John Legend's songs, 'I Can Change' and 'So High.' The entire 'Get Lifted' album is really a soundtrack to our love story, but to me, those were our best dates. Us riding around, dreaming about the future, but also having hard conversations and getting to the root of issues.

We spoke candidly about how we wanted our life together to be, and though I had previously said I would never date a man that had a child or children, it was his love and dedication to his daughter that drew me in even more.

Nothing beats the twenty plus hour road trip we endured when I helped him drive from Alabama to New York. This was one of those make or break moments, being cooped up in a car with someone for so long will really reveal if it's lust or love that you have for each other.

There's one incident that will stay with me forever. Prior to our engagement, Antoine was offered a dream job paying well over six figures. He turned it down without hesitation. His reason? It would require him to relocate to the west coast and he didn't want to be more than 4 hours away from his daughter . This sealed the deal. A man that was willing to turn down a quarter of a million dollars just to stay close to his child, left me speechless.

I remember smugly thinking that my dad would never do something like that for me. The Holy Spirit gently said to me, 'There are sacrifices your father has made that you know nothing about." Shocked, and a little taken aback, this statement stuck with me. I knew God wasn't condoning my father's actions, but what he did was give me a different point of view.

After processing this, I started to realize that people often don't know the gravity of the pain they've caused, so I started to have compassion for my father. My compassion didn't excuse my dad from his actions and responsibilities, but it freed me from carrying the burdens of his inability.

It was then that I knew my heart was in good hands. Being with someone who encourages you to look at things from a different perspective could change your entire outlook on life.

I had gotten to a point where I was tired of playing the blame game. I was tired of failed relationships. My mom would always say, "When you get sick and tired of being sick and tired, then you'll do something about it."

I also suggest you keep an ongoing journal. It'll help you chart your growth and can serve as a testimony to your deliverance. When you look back on it, you'll be able to see just how far you've come. My old journal entries from twenty-three years ago actually helped me write this book.

Go on a journey of self-discovery. You are not the sum of negative things that have happened to you. Instead, you are the compilation of every action that has gotten you to where you are now. Remember, it takes combining raw eggs, sugar, and flour to make a tasty cake. When some of those items are eaten on their own, it may not be appetizing, but when it's mixed all together, the results are delicious.

People like to say I'm going to forgive, but I'll never forget. I can testify that forgiveness allows you to remember without sorrow. You can look back on situations that once broke you and not feel the pain that was once so prevalent.

At this point in my life, I say if you're going to forgive, you might as well forget. Remember, one attribute of love is that it keeps no record of wrong. Faith overcomes feelings. Don't let your emotions manipulate you. They were given to you to enhance life, not to dictate it.

With some trepidation, I attended my biological father's funeral, and I'm so glad I did. I'm thankful to my cousin who traveled with me. Hard tasks don't seem as daunting when you have encouragement and help. Oddly enough, I found the service to be very comforting. I know that sounds weird, but it really was. I was able to hear many people speak on his behalf and share stories of how loving and generous he was to everyone in the community and those who crossed his path. I used to say that by choosing not to be in my life, my father missed out on having an amazing daughter, but after attending his funeral, I realized that, although flawed, he was a good man. Could he have done more for me? Heck yeah! But I'm very grateful for what he did.

One night I had a dream about him, and the Lord revealed to me the mindset behind my dad's decisions concerning me. He was in self-preservation and protection mode. It was too painful not to have all of me, so he had to detach himself totally. Ultimately, he decided that not being a part of my life was the best choice to not have to face his own pain.

Lack of accountability and avoidance are two telltale signs of a bastard and poverty mindset. They're closely linked.

Did you know you are the perfect combination of twenty-three chromosomes from your mother and twenty-three from your father? God knew who your parents would be before they were even born. The all-knowing God foresaw all the triumphs and trials in your life and still allowed for your birth. Why would He do that? Is it because He wanted you to suffer? No! It's because He knew you would be equipped to overcome any of life's obstacles that came your way.

And, while I'm on the subject of your strategically selected genetic composition, don't waste precious time wondering why you weren't born into another family or given different parents. If you switch out either parent for someone else, then there would be no you; the world would have been robbed of your uniqueness. There is no one else on earth that has your DNA. You are one of a kind.

God doesn't make carbon copies, even twins have their own distinct differences, so wishing you were someone else or trying to be someone else will only frustrate you and cause you to make decisions based on a corrupt desire. No one can beat you at being you, so work on being the best version of yourself that you can be.

What are you gifted at doing? What drives and motivates you? What is your purpose? What are your likes and dislikes? The answers to these questions will help you on your journey to self-discovery. Why be a watered-down version of someone else when you can be a top-shelf quality of yourself?

There's nothing more beautiful than confidence. Confidence comes from knowing who God has created you to be and what He's created you to do. People often spend more time dressing up their exterior and spend very little exploring what's inside of them. This causes a lot of pretty faces and empty hearts. Fluffed-up self-esteems based on the number of likes one gets on social media. But you're different. You're going to have substance. You're going to pursue God's purpose for you. You're going to have power!

Forgiveness is one of the keys to fulfillment.

Success and achievements are not the same as fulfillment. There are many successful people who aren't fulfilled. Like healing isn't the same as being made whole, or the equivalency of happiness to joy.

Not knowing your father isn't as detrimental as not knowing God. A relationship with Him is paramount to your quality of life. If you want the best that life has to offer, I urge you to invite Him into your heart and make Him your Lord.

Forgiving doesn't make you a doormat or naïve. It makes you smart and strong. What's the benefit of holding a grudge? Does it change anything? Forgiveness empowers you to stand up boldly in the face of what is trying to destroy you. That is what love does, that's what releasing does, that's what forgiveness does, that's what healing does. It gives YOU power.

After reading this book, you may find that my story is like yours, or you may think that the things that have happened to you were far worse. It really doesn't matter, because the fundamental steps to forgiveness are the same for all sizes and depths of hurt.

I've been healed and with that gift, I've made it my mission to help heal others, including you.

JOURNAL PROMPT:

What are the objects of your frustration? Do you know your triggers? We can't change what we won't admit. Once you can identify them, it'll be easier for you to resolve them. Feel free to write them down here:

Chapter X

Child of God

"You look just like your daddy." Have you ever heard that statement? I think there probably is nothing worse than hearing you look like the person you loathe. Or looking in the mirror and their features are all you can see. I mean, does God have a sense of humor or what?

I always admired my mother's silky hair, caramel skin, and tall frame. But here I am, a little on the short side, with thick hair and a deep brown complexion. Yup, you got it. Pretty much looking just like my daddy.

Growing up, I always felt a little different, but with no reference point of what was different about me, I suppressed those feelings and relished in the fact that at least this side of my family loved and supported me unconditionally.

Little did I know, my father's side of the family would be full of supportive and loving family members, too. I was introduced to one of my dad's sisters during a chance but Divine encounter, and she welcomed me into the fold.

When I met my paternal grandmother in 2010, I realized so much of my personality was indeed passed down genetically. Granny Bell, as I affectionately called her, was fiery and funny. Getting to know her helped to heal the broken little girl that was still inside of me. She said, "I ain't got to call Maury (Povich) for this one, when I first laid eyes on you, I knew you were mine." I laughed and wept; wept with my face in Granny's lap for what seemed like hours. The validation, the liberation, and the peace that overcame me still leave me speechless.

Also, remember my '98 Chevy Malibu? Well, on the days I drove past my father's house to get to the news station, my granny would say, "There goes my son's daughter on the way to work." When those around her would hear this, they simply thought that maybe due to her age she was mistaken. Granny knew all along. We still wouldn't meet for a few years later, but she knew, just like God knows who and where you are, too.

Sometimes the stone that the builders rejected turns out to be the cornerstone that bridges generations and becomes the physical embodiment of healing.

Even after this miraculous moment, my father still decided to not have a relationship with me. However, it couldn't be denied any longer that I was his seed. People would often stop me in stores because they thought they knew me. I chalked it up to a case of mistaken identity, but when Granny Bell showed me photos of my dad's siblings, I instantly knew why people would confuse me as his baby sister. I resemble her so much that it's almost scary.

I think it's typical for people to fantasize about what could've been instead of accepting what is, but what if God's allowance of your father's absence was really protection? The knowledge of this helped me to look at my upbringing from a place of gratitude instead of regret. I became grateful for the attributes my father's DNA played in my life. I promise you, if you look for something to express gratitude for, you'll find it.

"I knew you were mine." These words often ring in my ears, bringing a smile to my face and joy to my heart. It reminds me of God's declaration in the book of Jeremiah that says, "Before He formed us in our mothers' womb, He knew us'" (Jeremiah 1:5)! If God formed you and knows you, then what else do you need? It would be nice to know the familial history and not feel like a piece is missing, but in God is everything you need.

There are benefits of doing things God's way, and of course, there are consequences when we disobey. It is by design that his forgiveness of us is tied to our forgiveness of others. When it comes to identity, I'm no longer in crisis. I now realize that societal labels don't define me. God has called me many things and I associate myself with those over anything else. I encourage you to research and see what He's called you; I can assure you that bastard isn't one of them.

Being a child of God means that you have constant protection, provision, salvation, access, redemption, authority, dominion, and power. When we embody God's Spirit and adopt His ways, we positively impact the lives of others and align situations to His holy will. You'll begin to dominate your environment and life instead of them dominating you. The Kingdom of Heaven operates by a set of standards that is to be emulated here on Earth.

Above all else, I implore you to desire and cultivate a relationship with God. Through Jesus, we have access to benefits that only His sacrifice can give. Out of everything God created, you are His most prized possession. Live like it!

The Bible is filled with accounts of just how much God loves us. In the book of Psalms, it says, "If we were to count God's thoughts toward us, they would be more than grains of sand" (Psalm 139:17–18). Do you know how astronomical that must be? It is impossible to count every grain of sand, yet God's thoughts toward us outnumber them.

Earlier in the chapter, I spoke about the plight I felt looking like my dad, knowing that I didn't like him. I'm sure many of you can relate. Well, there's this guy I know who didn't meet his biological father until he was seventeen years old. Unfortunately, his father wasn't aware of his existence, but once he found out, he made a conscious effort to be a part of his son's life. I'm sure there are extenuating circumstances that would cause a mother to withhold the identity of her child's father, but I can't help but imagine that, ultimately, this does more harm than good. Could you imagine meeting your father for the first time at your high school graduation? Well, that's what happened to my friend. He didn't know his father would be in attendance, but as he was greeting his family after the graduation ceremony, he saw a man in the distance walking toward them.

Instantly and instinctively, my friend knew this had to be his dad. He could tell solely by the way he walked. I've had the pleasure of meeting his father, and I can't help but marvel at the similarities they share, from their stride to the cadence of their speech, their intellectual astuteness, mannerisms, shared interests, you name it.

I mentioned this story because this is how God wants us to be identified. When people see you, do you resemble the Creator? Do you act like you're a child of God?

What is a child of God anyway? That phrase gets mentioned a lot but allow me to expound for just a bit. Your bloodline matters. Recently I was watching a show about a royal family. The queen was upset that her sons had fathered over fifty illegitimate children but had no true heirs. Could you imagine having the blood of kings and queens coursing through your veins, but because your parents weren't married when you were conceived, you're subjected to living as a commoner?

At times, some illegitimate children were afforded certain privileges and a life of comfort, but they would never be eligible to rule or reign. They would never be in the line of succession for the throne. The denial of their birthright was determined by their conception.

This is the very reason Jesus came to earth. His entire mission was for the restoration of mankind. It's the blood of Jesus that gives access to God's throne and repairs the relationship between the Creator and His creation.

Genesis 1:26 tells us exactly why God created humans. It was to give us dominion of the earth and for us to rule over the earth like He rules heaven. When it says in John 3:16 that God so loved the world that he gave his only begotten son, the word world in this scripture doesn't mean globe, planet, or the inhabitants of it. In Greek, which is the original language the New Testament Bible is written, world means kosmos.

Kosmos is defined as order, arrangement, and original intent—to order or adorn, to put in order literally and figuratively. Essentially something that is well-arranged, that which has order or something arranged harmoniously.

So, that same scripture would read as, for God so loved his order, arrangement, original intent that he gave his only begotten Son. What did God give his Son to do? Most people would say for the forgiveness of our sins, which is true, but in addition to that, it was to give us access back to being heirs of God.

The sanctification of our sins through the blood of Jesus allows us to experience life as God had intended. Scripture tells us that we are a royal priesthood, a holy nation. When He says King of kings and Lord of lords in Revelation 19:16. God is the ultimate king and lord in heaven and we're supposed to be king and lords in the earth.

I know I've given scripture references before, but I wanted to dig a little deeper with this in hopes that it will truly show you God's plan and how the blood matters when it comes to legacy and royalty.

Romans 8:1–17 says it so clearly, "Therefore, there is now no condemnation for those who are in Christ Jesus, 2 because through Christ Jesus the law of the Spirit who gives life has set you[a] free from the law of sin and death. 3 For what the law was powerless to do because it was weakened by the flesh,[b] God did by sending his own Son in the likeness of sinful flesh to be a sin offering.[c] And so he condemned sin in the flesh, 4 in order that the righteous requirement of the law might be fully met in us, who do not live according to the flesh but according to the Spirit.

5 Those who live according to the flesh have their minds set on what the flesh desires; but those who live in accordance with the Spirit have their minds set on what the Spirit desires. 6 The mind governed by the flesh is death, but the mind governed by the Spirit is life and peace. 7 The mind governed by the flesh is hostile to God; it does not submit to God's law, nor can it do so. 8 Those who are in the realm of the flesh cannot please God.

9 You, however, are not in the realm of the flesh but are in the realm of the Spirit, if indeed the Spirit of God lives in you. And if anyone does not have the Spirit of Christ, they do not belong to Christ. 10 But if Christ is in you, then even though your body is subject to death because of sin, the Spirit gives life[d] because of righteousness. 11 And if the Spirit of him who raised Jesus from the dead is living in you, he who raised Christ from the dead will also give life to your mortal bodies because of[e] his Spirit who lives in you.

12 Therefore, brothers and sisters, we have an obligation—but it is not to the flesh, to live according to it. 13 For if you live according to the flesh, you will die; but if by the Spirit you put to death the misdeeds of the body, you will live.

14 For those who are led by the Spirit of God are the children of God. 15 The Spirit you received does not make you slaves, so that you live in fear again; rather, the Spirit you received brought about your adoption to sonship.[f] And by him we cry, *"Abba,*[g] Father." 16 The Spirit himself testifies with our spirit that we are God's children. 17 Now if we are children, then we are heirs—heirs of God and co-heirs with Christ, if indeed we share in his sufferings in order that we may also share in his glory." (NIV)

In Psalm 27, even David spoke of being forsaken by earthly parents but having comfort in knowing that he could never be rejected by God. I hope this serves as a source of reassurance for you too.

JOURNAL PROMPT:

What are your takeaway from this chapter?

Conclusion

Listen, I am passionate about protecting the innocence of children. In our society, I believe children grow up entirely too fast, oftentimes having to recover from the trauma of their parents' unprocessed pain. Because of this, I was determined to heal for my sanity, but most importantly, for the sake of my children. Trauma leaves traces of its existence; it's evident in how we think about ourselves and treat others.

Unresolved hurt can cause roadblocks to self-discovery, stunting growth, wasting precious years, and harming people along the way. Jesus tells us in Matthew 22:36–40 the two greatest commandments:

1. Love the Lord your God with all your heart, and with all your soul, and with all your mind. ' This is the greatest and first commandment.

2. And the second is like it: You shall love your neighbor as yourself.

This scripture never speaks specifically on how to love yourself, but in adhering to it, it allows God an opportunity to show what true love looks like. A relationship with God is reciprocal. The only reason we can even love Him is because He first loved us. He is the epitome of true relationship goals. You can never give Him anything and not get something in return. It's the simple principle of sowing and reaping. As you learn to love God with everything you have, He lavishes you with life-changing truth.

It's the commitment to doing the first part that makes the second part attainable. I didn't say it was easy, but God wouldn't have told us to do it if it couldn't be done. So many people say, "I love myself," but it's not evident in the choices they make. I believe we're loving ourselves the best we know how, but with God, there's always a better way.

The renowned Frederick Douglas poignantly stated that it is easier to build strong children than to repair broken men. This has become my life's mantra. You see, the thing about pain is that it can be generational, engrafted into our genetic makeup, influencing decisions even when we're not aware. I refuse to perpetuate this cycle, and I hope you'll make the decision to do the same.

The word bastard is a trope designed to negatively classify a certain group of people. It's intended to devalue a person based on circumstances that were outside of their control. However, your identity or self-worth should never come from external factors.

We weren't given options on who our parents would be; that decision was totally up to God. Nevertheless, the truth is, and will always remain, that you are God's choice, a part of His perfect plan, and there's no void too great where He can't rescue you.

You're not in this alone. In Malachi 4:6, God said that "He will turn the hearts of fathers to their children and the hearts of children to their fathers." You have supernatural help, all you have to do is take the first step.

Forgive.

CONCLUSION

A Prayer for You: (Say Aloud)

To the Father of fathers, the Creator of us all, God Almighty:

Thank you for choosing me. My birth was your idea and my parents were merely the vessels you used to get me into the earth. Show me why I was born and what I'm supposed to do with my life.

I trust that your plans for me are good. I come to You, the Restorer, Healer, and Redeemer, to help me exchange my bitterness and give me Your Divine perspective of my life.

With You, I know all things are possible to those who believe. Open my heart and mind to receive the truth. Wash me with your love and cover me with your blood. Give me experiences and proof that You are real and care for me.

Help me be mindful to only find my identity in your Word. I repent and renounce anything that is not of You.

You are God, and You are eternally good. I thank you for my life and for setting me free.

I pray this in the name that has all power and deserves all praise, Jesus the Christ. Amen!

Prayer Points and Prophetic Decrees:

Heavenly Father, any obstacle that's standing in the way of my forgiveness and healing, I ask you to reveal and remove it now.

Heavenly Father, give me the courage to face my deepest and darkest pain so that it will lose its power over me.

Heavenly Father, open the eyes of my heart so I may see myself the way you see me.

Heavenly Father, by Your Spirit and power, I uproot every deep-seated plot of the enemy to use my fatherlessness against me.

Heavenly Father, equip me with the grace needed to be committed to the process of transformation.

Heavenly Father, cancel any bloodline curses from my paternal and maternal sides of the family.

Heavenly Father, release all blessings attached to my bloodline because of the faith of the righteous.

I decree that every plot manufactured for my emotional, physical, or spiritual demise fails.

I decree that I am the beloved of God, highly cherished, protected, and provided for.

I detach myself from a bastard mindset

My intellect, will, and emotions are in alignment with the Word of God.

Where I have come into agreement with lies and deception, show me mercy.

In Christ, I have been made new.

Add to this list as you see fit, and don't stop until you get your breakthrough.